RECOVERY from REJECTION

YOUR GATEWAY TO FREEDOM

Ryan LeStrange

TABLE OF CONTENTS

1. Diagnosing the Problem … 1
2. Trauma and Wounds … 15
3. Jesus the Healer … 21
4. Responsibilities of Spiritual Fathers and Mothers … 45
5. The Law of Transfer … 51
6. Identity is Key … 59
7. Divine Remedies … 65

Recovery from Rejection
Copyright 2021 Ryan LeStrange
Published by LeStrange Global, LLC

All rights reserved. This book or any portion thereof may not be reproduced or used in any manner without permission of the publisher.

Cover Design: J.L. Design Creative Group

Scripture quotations marked NASB are from the NEW AMERICAN STANDARD BIBLE®, Copyright © 1960, 1962, 1963, 1968, 1971, 1972, 1973, 1975, 1977, 1995 by The Lockman Foundation. Used by permission (www.Lockman.org).

Scriptures marked KJV are taken from the KING JAMES VERSION (KJV): KING JAMES VERSION, public domain.

Scriptures marked NKJV are taken from the NEW KING JAMES VERSION (NKJV): Scripture taken from the NEW KING JAMES VERSION®. Copyright © 1982 by Thomas Nelson, Inc. Used by permission. All rights reserved.

Scriptures marked AMP are taken from the AMPLIFIED BIBLE (AMP): Scripture taken from the AMPLIFIED® BIBLE, Copyright © 1954, 1958, 1962, 1964, 1965, 1987 by the Lockman Foundation Used by Permission (www.Lockman.org).

Scripture quotations taken from the Amplified® Bible (AMPC), Copyright © 1954, 1958, 1962, 1964, 1965, 1987 by The Lockman Foundation Used by permission. www.Lockman.org

1
DIAGNOSING THE PROBLEM

I am sure we can all look back at our lives and identify a moment when we felt the sting of rejection. Maybe it was when we were young, and a secret crush did not share our affection. Or perhaps it was a playground game when we were the last one picked. It may have happened through an embarrassing moment or a word curse from an adult, sibling, or even a friend. Perhaps it was a traumatic relationship or a deep disappointment. Whatever the case, it is sure that at some moment, or perhaps several, you have experienced the pain of rejection, which always comes to make you feel inadequate, dismissed, or not good enough.

One of the things I've come to understand about the enemy is that he does not plan things randomly. He is very strategic. He plans his attacks, intending to shackle us in a place of pain, despair, and bondage. He wants to make you feel less than, inferior to others to keep you from fulfilling your potential. Rejection can be one of the most difficult pains to overcome. It camouflages itself to remain hidden beneath other emotions and experiences. It hides to avoid confrontation, exposure, and deliverance.

Rejection is a dangerous trap set to lead a person away from their God-given destiny and keep them bound in unnecessary pain. Even powerfully anointed people can experience cycles of dysfunction. They can bounce from relationship to relationship, blaming it all on the devil. Others have acute instability in their decision-making or leadership responsibilities. Both the emotional rejection and the demons attached to it must be recognized and dealt with properly. God can and does deliver with absolute authority and power. He has a wonderful ministry of healing, reaching, and restoring even the most broken and damaged soul. The first step is recognition.

For you have not received a spirit of slavery leading to fear again, but you have received a spirit of adoption as sons by which we cry out, "Abba! Father!" The Spirit Himself testifies with our spirit that we are children of God, and if children, heirs also, heirs of God and fellow heirs with Christ, if indeed we suffer with Him so that we may also be glorified with Him.

—Romans 8:15-17, NASB

Just as He chose us in Him before the foundation of the world, that we should be holy and without blame before Him in love, having predestined us to adoption as sons by Jesus Christ to Himself, according to the good pleasure of His will, to the praise of the glory of His grace, by which He made us accepted in the Beloved.

—Ephesians 1:4-6, NKJV

One of the most inspiring warriors in all of scripture is the valiant King David. He was a mighty man who led the armies of Israel in continual victory. He was known for both his strength and courage. There was no challenge from which David would run. He exuded confidence in God, his Father. However, David wasn't always in a position of power, and he, unfortunately, knew the depths of the sting of rejection.

> He also chose David His servant
> And took him from the sheepfolds;
> From the care of the ewes with suckling lambs He brought him
> To shepherd Jacob His people,
> And Israel His inheritance.
> So he shepherded them according to the integrity of his heart,
> And guided them with his skillful hands.
> — Psalm 78:70-72, NASB

David was tasked with an assignment typically reserved for a servant. His father and brothers left him tending the sheep on the backside of the hill. They thought him unworthy of any crucial or important responsibilities. Time and again in his life, he faced rejection from those closest to him, those who should have been his stoutest supporters. Imagine the pain of knowing that even your own family disregarded you, seeing no value in you. Despite this crushing pain, David found a place of solace in the presence of God. It was his tabernacle in the wilderness that brought David into a place of greatness. David learned from his time tending sheep how to be a shepherd of men. He had an exceptional reliance on God established through his discovery of the secret place. Instead of running from God in all the pain and despair, he ran toward the presence of the Father. His heart found comfort in the hands of his Creator. It was this intimate relationship with God that would catapult David to the highest place of power. He chose presence over pain! His life reveals a great example for us all.

In these verses, we read great hope in the midst of David's sorrow. God saw the faithfulness and integrity of David's heart and used these moments of difficulty to cultivate wisdom and faithfulness in his life. Many times, our vision is too short-sighted. We judge our life by a moment or a season, unable to see the hand of God working at the core of our struggle. God loves to orchestrate a comeback story. His favorite way to tell that story is through our lives. He moves in the broken places and the painful seasons. He uses these as His opportunity to cultivate our character, preparing us for the promotion that is to come. I would submit to you, the way we handle a difficult season determines the speed of our promotion. David passed the test and rose to another level.

We see the pattern of rejection surface again in the life of David when the prophet Samuel came to his father's house to anoint a king. In this moment of opportunity, every member of the family, except young David, was gathered to see who the next king would be. Unfortunately, his father could not see the potential in David's life. Instead, he chose to look through his own limited standards. God does not see things the way humans see. The prophet could not seem to find the future king in the house. Yet, urged by the Lord to keep looking, he called for the last remaining, the youngest son.

> And Samuel said to Jesse, "Are these all the children?" And he said, "There

> remains yet the youngest, and behold, he is tending the sheep." Then Samuel said to Jesse, "Send and bring him; for we will not sit down until he comes here."
> —1 Samuel 16:11, NASB

David was the underdog. He had been discounted and left out, yet God had big plans for his life. Let this message inspire you and bring you to a place of hope. God loves to rewrite the story of His children. In this instance, He validated and brought redemption to the purpose on David's life.

David's father requested him to take food and supplies to his brothers. As a dutiful son, he obeyed, being sent to the front lines of battle, and was again rejected and harassed by his brothers.

> Now Eliab his oldest brother heard when he spoke to the men; and Eliab's anger burned against David and he said, "Why have you come down? And with whom have you left those few sheep in the wilderness? I know your insolence

> and the wickedness of your heart; for you have come down in order to see the battle."
>
> —1 Samuel 17:28, NASB

They taunted him even in a moment when he was sent to serve them. Time and again, David had to overcome the rejection of his brothers and his father. It could not have been an easy thing for his heart to bear, but he found a way to persevere. I believe it was his worship life that was his secret weapon!

> For my father and mother have forsaken me, but the LORD will take me up.
>
> — Psalms 27:10, NASB

In these words, David expresses the pain he felt from the rejection he faced from those he loved. Yet, David's story did not end with pain and defeat; he relied upon God despite the odds stacked against him. David knew his God would not forsake him. He knew he must trust in God alone. God brought great victory in every area of his life and used him in a mighty way! He turned him from a victim to a warrior. His life is a testimony of recovery.

Unresolved rejection will grow like a festering wound. The spirit of rejection will take over a person's thought processes to twist their way of thinking. It incapacitates their ability to form healthy emotional and spiritual relationships. It will stall out their ability to grow and mature in the things of God and creates grave emotional instability. But there is an answer! A rejected soul can be healed, and the demons cast out, but the first step is identification.

How do I recognize rejection in my life? Let's look through manifestations of rejection so that we can properly identify it.

SYMPTOMS OF REJECTION

- **DEFENSIVE**

    Those battling the spirit of rejection instinctively respond defensibly. They are unable to handle constructive criticism or process normal conflicts. There is an undue need to defend themselves because of the lurking wound just beneath the surface.

- **EMOTIONAL WALLS**

  The spirit of rejection can create tremendous relational barriers as an act of self-preservation and protection. In order to avoid the potential of being hurt, a person operating in rejection creates distance between themselves and others. They avoid intimate relationships. They only have relationships with well-maintained walls to avoid letting anyone in too close. While emotional boundaries are healthy, excessive walls and barriers are not.

- **DISTANT**

  A spirit of rejection causes a person to be emotionally isolated. They become distant from others. They can be in a space yet not be emotionally present. They are self-guarded.

- **EMOTIONAL TURMOIL**

  The deep wounds inflicted by this spirit cause emotional turbulence in the life of a person battling rejection. The least little conflict or challenge can open the floodgates of emotions. The pain resurfaces.

- **DRAMA**
  Anytime there are demon powers and emotional wounds in operation, there is potential for unnecessary drama. Human relationships can be challenging and include a plethora of human emotions. However, healthy ones maintain normal levels of conflict resolution. A person bound with rejection is often very quick to fly off the handle or burst into tears without a valid reason.

- **UNHEALTHY AND UNSTABLE RELATIONSHIPS**
  A person bound with the spirit of rejection will have great difficulty engaging in healthy relationships. It does not mean they won't have relationships; it simply means they will not have healthy ones. Depending on the makeup of the person or people they are in relationship with, their relationships can be unstable. They often run from conflict and are quick to break covenant with other people as a form of self-preservation.

- **EXCESSIVE CONTROL AND MANIPULATION**
  Deliverance and healing from emotional trauma are necessary because, if left unresolved, it can lead to

severe spiritual and emotional issues. Often people who have not conquered rejection become domineering and controlling. Rejection can become an open door for manipulative demons to operate through a person, wreaking havoc on the lives of others.

When Saul was rejected from his place of leadership by the Lord, he turned into a tormented and controlling leader. Saul sought to attack David, who carried the fresh anointing of God. In the early days of Saul's life, he loved the presence of God and valued the anointing of the Holy Spirit. Yet, when he became a demonized individual bound by rejection, he fought the anointing of God, persecuting the carrier of that anointing. Not confronting rejection in your life is dangerous, leading to demonic behavior patterns.

While many of these symptoms are broad and possibly experienced by the average person, you must take a quick inventory of this checklist. If you identify with these characteristics, take a moment to pause and reflect. Ask yourself if you may be battling a spirit of rejection. Have you overlooked old soul wounds that need to be healed? Do you need a fresh touch of God in your mind and emotions to deliver you from these pains?

2
TRAUMA AND WOUNDS

I remember clearly when the Spirit of the Lord began to speak to me about soul trauma. I had a strong leading to begin teaching the people of God about the value of a healed soul and normalizing their thought patterns. God opened revelation to me regarding the strongholds the enemy sets up in the human mind. As I came into a greater understanding of these principles, one question remained on my mind. How do we lead people to healing? I was expecting a deep and mysterious formula, but instead, I got a very simple answer. The Lord simply told me to lead them to Him! That just seemed too simple for me. Then He began to unveil Himself to me in scripture as the Healer of the brokenhearted and the one who restores our soul.

> The Lord is near to the brokenhearted and saves those who are crushed in spirit.
>
> — Psalm 34:18, NASB

I love this psalm assuring us that He is near to the brokenhearted. One of the intents of trauma is separation. The traumatic event or episode seeks to separate people, preventing them from healthy connections with other people. Another work of unresolved trauma can be a sense of separation from the presence of the Lord. This comes from emotional issues and demonic influences that enter our lives at the point of trauma.

Often, traumatic episodes become a catalyst for shame and rejection. As human beings, we overestimate the power of the enemy and struggle in these moments to see the goodness of God. Our mind swirls with thoughts of God's abandonment as we find ourselves feeling disconnected from the life-giving presence of God. One of the symptoms of a spiritual attack is a feeling of the absence of the presence of God. The enemy knows that the presence of God acts as a weapon in our lives. When His glory is in our midst, it repels demonic entities. We are refreshed in God's glory. We are healed in God's glory. We are renewed in God's glory.

Anger and frustration following trauma can also cause a sense of separation from God's presence. On the other side of horrific emotional turmoil, we can easily fall into the blame game. Unfortunately, human beings often struggle with the question of why me? These issues cause people to search for an answer when often there is no clear explanation. We know the Bible tells us that every good and perfect gift comes from the Father of lights (James 1:17). To be more precise, good things come to our lives from God, and evil things bringing pain, torment, and discouragement come from the bowels of hell, inspired by the devil. This seems to be an easy truth to grasp, yet in times of vicious attack, the enemy accuses God, our Father, in our minds. Left unresolved, these types of mental attacks can have us believing God authored the tragedy that occurred in our life. That singular thought can lead to a great separation which only further fuels heaviness.

God, as the good Father, understands our questions, our doubts, and even our fears. He is constantly there for us with His loving hand and guidance in the most difficult of times. Should we be deceived in believing that God authored the hellacious episode in our life, we lose confidence in His ability to protect and preserve us. I believe that amid the deepest trials, we can find the stillness of His voice in a way that sustains us. We can also come to a place of clarity, understanding that it was indeed the enemy's work that brought about the attack. We must take a personal inventory, evaluating our decisions that may have contributed to any calamity. Having come to a place of restful confidence in God, we are set free to trust Him with our heart, mind, and life. It is in that place of trust that trauma is resolved and we are led back to the healing arms of our Father.

> He heals the brokenhearted
> And binds up their wounds.
> — Psalm 147:3, NASB

It is in His presence that we are made whole. We must understand that healing is different than mere surviving, which simply means that you are still alive. It is possible to live but not fully thrive spiritually or emotionally. It's possible to go through life in auto mode, existing but not feeling, engaging but not opening your heart, connecting but never fully trusting. While supportive friends can be a tremendous asset in a time like this, they cannot provide the needed healing. While a great counselor or therapist can be a highly effective tool in recovery, they cannot provide the healing. I advocate all these things during trauma or on the other side of a calamity. Yet, there is one thing that stands above all these methods: the healing presence of Almighty God.

When the Lord began to speak to me about emotional healing, He reinforced over and over establishing the concept of His divine healing ministry in the minds of His people. We must bring people to the place of the presence of the Father, and we must teach them how to open their hearts for the administration of His healing flow. The secret to recovery is in His presence! This is the secret to well-being! This is the secret to victorious living!

3
JESUS THE HEALER

> The Spirit of the Lord is upon me, because he hath anointed me to preach the gospel to the poor; he hath sent me to heal the brokenhearted, to preach deliverance to the captives, and recovering of sight to the blind, to set at liberty them that are bruised.
>
> —Luke 4:18, KJV

In this inaugural message of the Lord Jesus, He could have chosen any biblical concept to disclose, but he began by revealing Himself as the Healer of the brokenhearted. I have learned through the years that you cannot access an anointing that you do not recognize. I'm afraid that often, Christians overlook the anointing of Jesus to heal brokenhearted people. He has a mandate and a ministry commissioned by the Father to bring emotional healing to the lives of His people. Think about it for a moment; if your emotions remain unhealed, it's like a dam preventing the flow of God from moving freely in your life. The emotional walls create barriers in your relationships, becoming lodging points for the spirit of rejection.

The strategy of the enemy is to embed unresolved pain and conflict in our hearts. It's one thing to go through a battle or a trauma, but it's another thing to be completely healed. To be healed means that all the pain associated with the trauma has been removed. The burden has been loosed. The resultant thought patterns are broken, and a new way of thinking is established.

> Keep and guard your heart with all vigilance and above all that you guard, for out of it flow the springs of life.
> —Proverbs 4:23, AMPC

> Let not thine heart decline to her ways, go not astray in her paths. For she hath

cast down many wounded: yea, many strong men have been slain by her. Her house is the way to hell, going down to the chambers of death.

—Proverbs 7:25-27, KJV

Create in me a clean heart, O God; and renew a right spirit within me.

—Psalm 51:10, KJV

All three of these verses deal with our hearts and our responsibility to protect that part of our lives. When we think of the heart, we think of the physical organ beating in our chest. The Lord is not speaking here of our heart as an organ. He is speaking to the portion of our mind, which contains the decision-making faculties and the seat of our moral conscious. If that deep portion of our mind is contaminated and broken, everything that flows through it will be corrupted. So, we are commissioned to govern our soul. One of the first steps to healing from trauma is to take responsibility for your own well-being. You simply cannot delegate your emotional health to the hands of another. You couldn't help the trauma that assaulted your life, but you can decide to initiate the healing process.

How does this impact the work of rejection in our lives? It's quite simple: left alone, these pains foster patterns in our minds that are UN-healed. That un-healed place contaminates our relationships and decisions. It becomes a nest for demonic entities to torment and harass us. Healing and deliverance are two of the most vital ministries of Jesus. When it comes to emotional pain, He wants to minister both healing and deliverance to our lives.

> And Jesus went about all Galilee, teaching in their synagogues, and preaching the gospel of the kingdom, and healing all manner of sickness and all manner of disease among the people.
>
> And his fame went throughout all Syria: and they brought unto him all sick people that were taken with diverse diseases and torments, and those which were possessed with devils, and those

which were lunatick, and those that had
the palsy; and he healed them.
— Matthew 4:23-24, KJV

When we look at the ministry of Jesus, we see Him healing the sick and delivering the oppressed. Today's ministry world often separates these two vital ministries. I mean that some people will be drawn to the ministry of healing, while they may shun the ministry of deliverance. Conversely, some love the ministry deliverance but seldom focus on the ministry of healing. This is contradictory to the nature of Jesus, who operated in both of these needed ministries. He had compassion on both the bound and the sick, healing them all. I believe this example should provide hope in emotional healing and deliverance from the spirit of rejection.

One of the things I have learned on my journey with the Lord about emotional healing is to focus on His anointing to heal. We must have a strong revelation of who He is in our personal lives. We must have faith founded upon the written Word of God. We must have insight into His nature of goodness and kindness towards us. Think about it for a moment, would you trust an angry person with your brokenness? Would you be drawn to someone who was constantly mad at you and pour out your heart that needed to be mended? The answer is absolutely not! This is why you need to have a proper understanding of the current ministry of Jesus in your life. The best way to know what He wants to do is to look at what He did and who He is.

Jesus did not turn away the afflicted or the tormented. He called them to Himself. The Bible boldly declares that He is the same yesterday, today, and forever, meaning that He is still doing today whatever He was doing in the Bible. He is still compassionate towards the broken. He still longs to minister to the afflicted. His power is available right now to heal all manner of emotional pain and trauma. One of the most critical steps of recovery from rejection, distress, trauma, or fear is recognizing the abundant power of the Lord Jesus Christ available to you in every area of your soul!

You must be willing to come to Him and allow His healing touch to overwhelm you. You must be bold in your pursuit of the healing ministry of Jesus. You must unashamedly bring your wounds before the throne of grace and allow the oil of recovery to be poured upon your life. In worship, you must call upon the name of Jesus, who is your Deliverer and your Healer! You must resist the devil and tell him he has to flee from your life! You must break every tie to past pain and trauma as you open yourself up to the healing power of God.

COMMON EMOTIONAL WOUNDS

I want to look at some common wounds of the heart, hurts that partner together, inviting in a spirit of rejection. Many times, we are so busy that we fail to stop and take inventory of our emotional temperature. We may be at a boiling point, yet we fail to realize it because we're moving at a hurried pace. Times of quiet and reflection, along with daily devotion time, are so necessary in allowing the Lord to strengthen us through His Word and prayer.

In addition to rejection, these are all common wounds experienced in our emotions.

- **DEATH AND GRIEVING**

    Death is a natural part of life. In fact, for a believer, death can be a great reward. The Bible says to be absent from the body is to be present with the Lord. When a believer ceases to live on this earth, they immediately pass into the place of glory with the Lord Himself. It takes a renewed mind to understand and comprehend this transition properly. I certainly do not advocate abandoning the normal process of grieving as it is an absolute necessity when you lose someone you love. It is vital to accurately understand how the heart heals and how the mind recovers from such an episode. While one must embrace the normal process of grieving, one must also refuse to allow depression, heaviness, or weariness to set in. Even in this process, they must go to the Lord as the source of healing and deliverance.

- **DISAPPOINTMENT**

Unfortunately, disappointment is a part of the life experience. There may be something that you wanted, desired, or even believed for, but it did not come to pass. The enemy will use these times of frustration to sow seeds of discouragement in your heart and thought life. Sometimes we don't slow down long enough to thoroughly pray through a disappointment.

> I have been through times of great challenge and adversity, and when I stopped to reflect on what the Lord was speaking, He showed me that it was for my good. When He shut the door, He was protecting me, not rejecting me. One of the things that will help us navigate the pathway of disappointment is understanding the sovereignty of God.

> And we know that all things work together for good to them that love God, to them who are the called according to his purpose.
> —Romans 8:28, KJV

This verse brings great freedom into your life as you realize that God is still working in every mountain and valley. He is working when the door opens, and He is working when the door closes! It is a matter of learning to trust Him and relinquish the pain of disappointment to Him so He can heal you.

- **UNFULFILLED DESIRES AND DREAMS**

    Each of us is born with the capacity to believe, to hope, and to dream. God inspires dreams and gives us a hope for the future. Part of the walk of faith is learning to believe God for opportunities and adventures.

    There are times when our desires may not be realized, or a dream does not come to pass as we thought it would. It is in those moments that our faith is challenged, and we must rely upon the grace of God to reassure our footing. The enemy uses these times in an attempt to knock us off the pathway with pressure, pain, or guilt, but we must stand steadfast in the knowledge of God's goodness and love, despite what we see or are experiencing!

- **BROKEN RELATIONSHIPS**

    Part of the human experience is the intersection of lives, experiences, and emotions as people connect. Some relationships are forever, and then some relationships are for a season. There are relationships in which both parties appropriately value and steward the relationship, and there are those that are not cherished or protected. Sometimes in our life, when there is a relationship shift, there is also great pain. We may not know how to process wounds of a disconnect or messy breakup. We may find ourselves conflicted about the ending of a seasonal relationship. When a relationship ends, there is a specific measure of pain. If this type of grief is not handled healthily, it can open the door for further emotional turbulence and trauma.

- **OFFENSES**

    A brother offended is harder to be won over than a strong city, and [their] contentions separate them like the bars of a castle.

    —Proverbs 18:19, AMPC

It is impossible to do life with people without having struggles. There is both a healthy and an unhealthy way to resolve conflict. Part of the maturing process is learning how to handle disagreements in a biblical manner and, as a believer, keep a strong witness. There are times someone may wrong you, and offense tries to grab hold of you. An offense can become a spiritual cancer and an open door for demonic entities to find a resting place. Forgiveness is the answer to slam the door of offense shut in our lives. We must make a decision to forgive. This does not always mean relinquishing needed boundaries, that the relationship resumes as before, or that the person still has the same position in your circle as previously. It is possible to forgive a person but maintain a boundary for your own emotional and spiritual health.

- **NO LONGER ORPHANS**

    There is a rest and confidence that comes into our lives when we know and understand God's great love and care for us as sons and daughters. The enemy does a tremendous job trying to talk us out of our true identity and saturate our minds with lies. The cross was the ultimate place of restoration as Jesus gave it all to bring us into the family of God.

His blood paved the way for us to become new creations. We are no longer orphans! We are now the sons and daughters of the living God. This truth obliterates the powers of darkness that attempt to bind us in fear and rejection. We are set free from the grasp of Satan by the knowledge of God and His great love for us.

We must settle in our hearts our new position in Christ Jesus! We must no longer allow the enemy to sow seeds of deception into our minds. An orphan heart will bind us in a cycle of unhealthy relationships and unrealized potential. I have often witnessed powerfully gifted people live in a state of spiritual and emotional paralysis because of rejection and abandonment. The orphan heart shut down their fruitful service in the kingdom of God and brought them to a standstill! This mindset makes it very difficult to form meaningful relationships, serve alongside gifted leaders, or receive from those God has placed in our lives. In every case, the orphan heart is the result of rejection or past trauma. An orphan heart lacks the revelation of Abba's love and acceptance.

> And he will [himself] go before Him in the spirit and power of Elijah, to turn back the hearts of the fathers to the children, and the disobedient and incredulous and unpersuadable to the wisdom of the upright [which is the knowledge and holy love of the will of God]–in order to make ready for the Lord a people [perfectly] prepared [in spirit, adjusted and disposed and placed in the right moral state].
>
> —Luke 1:17, AMPC
>
> *—see also Isaiah 40:3; Malachi 4:5-6.*

This prophetic promise brought directly from heaven through Gabriel reveals the heart of the Father. Before He ever created a church or an organization, He instituted a family. It was His desire to live in union with Adam and Eve, but the devil had another plan. The enemy came to deceive Adam and Eve, to disrupt the family of God, and to break their unity and fellowship with God. He was a trespasser with no legal rights to Adam and Eve. His only tool was deception in order to form a rebellious desire in the hearts of God's children that would cause them to break covenant with their Father. Unfortunately, his plan was successful, and humanity was thrown into a crisis that only the blood of Jesus could solve.

It has always been the plan of God that the kingdom looks like a family. This is a twofold revelation. It begins with having a strong identity as sons and daughters utterly in love with their Father! Religious demons will make the kingdom about rules and regulations, forgetting the importance of relationships. These spirits bind people in lifeless cycles void of power and intimacy. God wants to relate to His children as their ultimate Protector, Provider, and Father.

The second dimension of family that I believe God is clarifying in the above verse is the functioning of the church as a family with strong spiritual fathers and mothers, birthing sons and daughters for effective service in the kingdom of God. This work is at the forefront of the coming move of God and demands our attention to the healing ministry of Jesus. We must declare these truths and allow the Spirit of the Lord to move into the hearts of broken men and women, breaking the shackles of rejection and past trauma. There is a glorious freedom in Christ Jesus that obliterates the powers of hell. When the people of God are healed, relationships are stronger, and the flow of God is rich.

> For [the Spirit which] you have now received [is] not a spirit of slavery to put you once more in bondage to fear, but you have received the Spirit of adoption [the Spirit producing sonship] in [the bliss of] which we cry, Abba (Father)! Father!
>
> The Spirit Himself [thus] testifies together with our own spirit, [assuring us] that we are children of God.
> — Romans 8:15-16, AMPC

The precious Holy Spirit has been sent on assignment to break the spirit of slavery from our lives. He has come to bring forth the Spirit of adoption and produce sonship. How can we relate to a kingdom leader as a spiritual father or mother if we have a false concept of God's role in our lives? The answer is simple; we cannot. Therefore, we become trapped in an endless cycle of ineffective relationships and broken alignments. When we focus on earthly relationships without prioritizing our primary relationship with our heavenly Father, we miss the mark. We must learn how to be sons and daughters with absolute trust and confidence in our Father. We rest in the fact that He is our provider, protector, defender, healer, and deliverer. We must also know that He is a good Father who is not angry with us but in love with us. He desires to give us good gifts and provide that for which we have need. We can trust Him with our very lives.

Unresolved rejection and pain make these truths impossible to understand and accept. This is why we need the ministry of the Holy Spirit as declared in the above verses. As we yield to praying in the Spirit, we are fellowshipping with the Master Teacher, who was there from the very beginning and origin of time itself. Holy Spirit is the one with infinite wisdom and understanding, boundless love and compassion for us, and just judgment and righteous decrees. Every moment spent in the presence of Holy Spirit leads us to divine transformation from the inside out. As we pray in the Spirit, mysteries are unraveled bit by bit and line by line. The Holy Spirit unfolds and reveal truth to us! The knowledge of the truth makes us free and sets us on a brand-new course. The Holy Spirit's job description is to deliver us from abandonment and bring us to the full understanding of our total and complete adoption.

- **APOSTOLIC FAMILIES**

    One of the steps we must take in ministry is to shift from an organizational mindset to that of an apostolic family. While the apostolic demands precise administration and in-depth plans for growth, the center is the relationship with sons and daughters. Apostolic ministry is not a pyramid scheme with the leader sitting on top disconnected from those serving. At its highest, apostolic ministry produces sons and daughters, releases impartation, and sends them on assignment. In order to engage this level of function, we must shift our mindset and get delivered from past wounds.

    Those attempting to serve in the kingdom of God and still struggling with an orphan heart will display certain attributes. They will be unusually defensive because they have had to be self-protectors and providers. They view relationships opportunistically. They have difficulty cultivating covenant relationships. They find accountability abhorrent, shouting control anytime a leader requires submission. Don't get me wrong. I know there are controlling leaders who function as dictators and not fathers, which is a part of the problem. For the sake of this writing, I am not addressing that as much as I'm addressing the orphan nature in potential sons and daughters. Those carrying the orphan mentality engage in a false form of submission driven by ulterior motives. They will submit in name only to gain access to opportunity, but there exists a seed of rebellion dwelling in their hearts.

Spiritual orphans engage in a counterfeit form of prophetic ministry that is mean-spirited, void of any love. This type of prophetic people enjoy controversy and stirring strife in the name of the prophetic. They lack the love of the Father! They often seek out teachers, prophets, or other spiritual leaders whose messages are laced with a hint of rebellion and a strong spirit of independence because they also carry an orphan heart.

These individuals view ministry as an opportunity, not a place of covenant or family. They quickly disconnect from a ministry that requires covenant living, mature accountability, and enduring commitment. A place like this causes their hidden demons to manifest. They're drawn to teaching that justifies a lone ranger theology and nullifies dependence on other members of the body of Christ as proclaimed in scripture. These orphans spend more time blasting than building and love to identify problems without solutions.

One of the lasting results of abandonment and orphanhood is a lack of knowledge on being a true son or daughter. Many times, because of the breakdown in their natural family, there is a void of understanding in people's hearts concerning connection to a spiritual family; the side effect of a broken society and a false set of values established by a world system. In rightly discerning the word of truth concerning spiritual families, we must dig and study the roles of spiritual fathers and mothers and sons and daughters. Let's begin by examining some of the key components of sonship. What should spiritual sons and daughters do in a relationship with their fathers and mothers?

Five key qualities of sons and daughters:

1. **Listen**. Access is a sign of relationship. Whoever has access, you heed, listen, relate to, and give them influence in your life.
2. **Value.** Don't take the spiritual relationship lightly. Place great value on it. We invest in and pursue those we value.
3. **Honor**. Demonstrate honor through time investment, support, attention, acts of kindness, and sowing. You don't drink from a well that you have not sown into.
4. **Represent**. True sons and daughters reflect spiritual fathers and mothers. One of our highest demonstrations of sonship to Abba is reflecting His nature.
5. **Obey**. Obedience brings a blessing. One of the distinctions of a spiritual relationship is the choice to listen and obey instruction.

In everything that we are called to do in the kingdom of God, there is the divine ability granted to us by our Father. We can sometimes refer to this ability as the anointing, which is God's super on our natural. We can also refer to this ability as grace, which is divine ability bestowed upon us when we come into alignment with the will of God for our life. With this in mind, I want to examine some of the graces upon a spiritual son or daughter.

GRACES OF A SON OR DAUGHTER

GRACE OF IDENTITY
DNA—it is reproduced! Sons RE-Present the Father.

GRACE TO SERVE
As God's children, we are graced and empowered to serve Him. When God connects us to spiritual fathers and mothers, we can serve—not just by natural means but by spirit and bond.

GRACE TO INHERIT!
Sonship always releases inheritance, a huge spiritual principle that brings another dimension of divine power. Impartation is also a sonship blessing. There is a spiritual inheritance!

GRACE TO ENDURE AND PERSEVERE
Perhaps one of the greatest indicators of a son or daughter is that they are faithful! This stability does not come

without challenge, but a true son or daughter is found faithful and enduring to the end.

GRACE TO HONOR

Sons show honor. Sons of God honor the Father with obedience, which is a mark of honor.

> If ye love me, keep my commandments.
> — John 14:15, KJV

> But I hope in the Lord Jesus to send Timothy to you shortly, so that I also may be encouraged when I learn of your condition. For I have no one *else* of kindred spirit who will genuinely be concerned for your welfare. For they all seek after their own *interests*, not those of Christ Jesus. But you know of his proven worth, that he served with me in the furtherance of the gospel like a child *serving* his father. Therefore I hope to send him immediately, as soon as I see how things *go* with me; and I trust in the

> Lord that I myself will also be coming shortly.
>
> — Philippians 2:19-24. NASB

Due to the deep level of relationship and the measure of impartation released into his life, Paul was able to trust Timothy with the most valuable aspects of his apostolic work. Timothy was able to go as his ambassador to the churches and congregations under Paul's apostolic care. In the structure of a family, this sincere trust should be a normal dimension of apostolic ministry.

Spiritual sonship is certainly not a one-sided relationship. A spiritual son or daughter should have a healthy and balanced relationship with their spiritual mother and father. While it is easy to outline expectations of a relationship, the reality is that no two relationships are exactly alike. There is a whole range of variables based upon the parties' unique callings, abilities, and personalities. With that in mind, let's examine some general characteristics of spiritual fathers and mothers.

4
RESPONSIBILITIES OF SPIRITUAL FATHERS AND MOTHERS

LOVE

The foundation, the root system, of every covenant relationship is love. There must be a God-ordained love that keeps both parties cemented in compassion, commitment, and forgiveness towards one another.

GUIDE

A relationship with the right spiritual father or mother, whether through teaching, one-on-one counsel, or other aspects of a relationship, should guide the spiritual son or daughter. Again, remember that each relationship is unique. Some relationships will be more personable than others, but the commitment in and of itself will offer a measure of supernatural guidance. It is an unlocking type of relationship that opens up realms of destiny.

GOVERN

Perhaps one of the most controversial dimensions of both apostolic relationships and spiritual sons and daughters is governance. Governing represents authority. Where there is authority, government and healthy boundaries are established. A spiritual mother or father must be able to say no to their son or daughter without retribution or anger! Correction should never be motivated by control or insecurity but with love and wisdom. Every leader needs a leader!

PRAY

Prayer is a key attribute of all covenant relationships. Throughout my years of ministry, I have found that it is impossible for me to remain offended with someone when I'm praying for them daily. Prayer unlocks grace!

Prayer unlocks wisdom! Prayer unlocks favor! These relationships demand prayer; both parties praying for each other daily.

MENTOR

Mentors are not exclusively spiritual mothers or fathers. The role of mentorship is to educate and activate. A mentor brings you to another level in your spiritual development! You may have many mentors who are not spiritual fathers or mothers to you. However, an authentic spiritual parent, by example, will provide a level of mentorship that is life-changing.

IMPART

All covenant relationships empower a dimension of impartation. It is impossible to think about the apostolic ministry without recognizing the role of impartation. Simply put, God connects us to the right people to establish spiritual gifts, anointing, and levels of increase.

LEAD

A good spiritual mother or father confers leadership, including much-needed direction and wisdom. We can follow the example of our spiritual parents as they are following the example of Christ.

INVEST

Spiritual fathers and mothers invest in those they lead, which is natural in a healthy spiritual relationship. They support through teaching and preaching, with prayer and impartation, and by assisting in ministerial development.

CORRECT AND REBUKE

These two words are often corrupt in the modern church. There is no covenant relationship without correction or rebuke. When we submit to the Lord, we welcome His correction in our lives, understanding that it is because He loves us. The same should be said for a spiritual father or mother. Though a stern rebuke may hurt our feelings for a moment, we must understand that it has the potential to save us from an error that could damage our long-term destiny. Those battling the spirit of rejection will often view correction as control. Don't get me wrong; there are controlling leaders with unhealthy relationships. However, in the context of a healthy relationship, correction and rebuke are not dispensed to make you feel insignificant or unworthy but to save you from a wrong turn. With their experience and ministerial understanding, a good spiritual father or mother should see things that you cannot see. There must be a level of trust in which you receive from them speaking into your life even when it may not feel good at the moment but has long-term preservation for you.

FORGIVE

No matter how strong or wise a spiritual parent is or how good your relationship with them is, the bond will be tested. In developing arising ministers filled with zeal, a gifted entrepreneur with many ideas, or any other called person, mistakes are made as they navigate the call upon their life. These mistakes can frustrate a spiritual father or mother, irritating them at times. The relationship must be secure in the covenant love that has been established between both parties. Love empowers forgiveness! When we forgive, we let go of the wrongs committed. When we forgive, we are not constantly replaying what happened in the past, nor are we harboring bitter feelings. A good spiritual father or mother must forgive their spiritual son and daughter when mistakes are made and have an honest conversation and times of prayer to move forward.

LEAD WITH LOVE AND COMMITMENT

We end this section by again examining love, the principal thing. I am restating this because it is vital in this type of relationship. When there is love present, there is also commitment. There should never be a feeling between the two parties that the relationship could end at any moment. Now, I want to say something here that can be challenging; some relationships are seasonal. I reject the concept of a person frequently bouncing from spiritual relationships because of mood swings or offenses! I wholeheartedly believe these relationships are meant to be long-term. There are times when a believer may be growing in their calling and identity, and this growth requires a redefinition of existing relationships. I do not believe this should be a frequent thing in the context of spiritual mothers and fathers. Therefore, I believe that these relationships should have a long-term commitment creating a sense of security for all parties involved.

5
THE LAW OF TRANSFER

> A good man leaves an inheritance to his children's children, and the wealth of the sinner is stored up for the righteous.
> —Proverbs 13:22, NASB

It is hard for the human mind to grasp that one generation's obedience can cause the blessing to be passed down to the next generation or even further generations. Throughout the Word of God, we see that those who kept covenant with God secured blessing for their descendants. When God came to Abraham, He made a promise to his descendants, which is still working in the earth today!

There are covenant principles that must be understood to effectively empower relationships and shatter the lens of rejection in our lives. When we fully understand that the Father has accepted us, we are empowered to operate in covenant with Him, receiving His blessings and walking in our true identity. This realization then empowers us to form healthy covenant relationships that bring divine transfer into our lives. A transfer is the release of spiritual gifting, supernatural power, wisdom, and grace in divine ability from one party to another. God ordained relationships established and position us for a divine transfer. God never sends us to an assignment without releasing the ability and power to succeed. One of His transportation systems to move the force of favor and anointing from one person to another is impartation. Historically, God has transferred promises, mantels, and destinies from one generation to the next.

> Only give heed to yourself and keep your soul diligently, so that you do not forget the things which your eyes have seen and they do not depart from your heart

> all the days of your life; but make them
> known to your sons and your grandsons.
> —Deuteronomy 4:9, NASB

Spiritual fathers and mothers should transfer and impart wisdom. One of their job descriptions is to release their history with God and the lessons they've learned to the next generation. I never will forget the intimate conversations I had early in ministry with my spiritual father. He had been part of some of the great moves of God of his day. He saw the challenges and mistakes and the opportunities and breakthroughs of his colleagues. He shared his knowledge with me to prepare me to navigate my own ministry! I have often thought back on those conversations and the insight he transferred to me, which has safeguarded me through the years.

Transfer is the release of a spiritual gift, influence, or anointing.

> For I long to see you so that I may impart some spiritual gift to you, that you may be established.
> —Romans 1:11, NASB

The Apostle Paul was excited to see the church at Rome, not just to preach but to transfer. He was ready to pour from his apostolic mantle into every person's life connected to his assignment; this is a vital principle of the apostolic ministry. Relationship creates a catalyst for flow! Whatever we connect to flows over our lives and brings a divine transfer. Often, when we are praying to go to the next level, God will bring some next-level people into our lives to supernaturally empower us. We must break the chains of rejection to properly connect with the right people, at the right season, and for the right plans. A transfer is made through connection! The stronger the connection, the greater the flow!

> The Lord therefore said to Moses, "Gather for Me seventy men from the elders of Israel, whom you know to be the elders of the people and their officers and bring them to the tent of meeting, and let them take their stand there with you. Then I will come down and speak with you there, and I will take of the Spirit who is upon you, and will put

> Him upon them; and they shall bear the
> burden of the people with you, so that
> you will not bear it all alone.
> —Numbers 11:16-17, NASB

Moses had hit a lid in his leadership organization. God's answer was establishing a new structure that included divine relationships, levels of authority and assignment, and supernatural impartation. The first observation from these verses is that God appointed Moses to gather the people. He trusted Moses' wisdom and insight to properly identify those who had been faithful and committed in His assignment. I believe sometimes we over-spiritualize things and expect God to do all the work when He has granted us wisdom to discern and define our relationships. There will be a different expectation from a spiritual father or mother than from a friend. You can never direct a thing that has not been properly defined.

Moses gathered those whom he knew had been faithful and brought them into the presence of the Lord! A good leader draws you to a deeper presence and intimacy with God. Once they were brought forth,

God said He would take the Spirit upon Moses and put it upon them. It's interesting to me that He did not say He would activate their individual ministry but that He would take the flow that was on the life of Moses and put it on them; this is a transfer in operation. God connects spiritual sons and daughters to a mother or father. They are united in the anointing, in the mission, and in the overall assignment. While each son or daughter has their unique calling, they are part of a much bigger picture. They are called to labor in the gospel, alongside their apostolic father or mother. Rebels refuse this concept, becoming offended by this type of conversation. Yet, it's in the Word of God. We often enter into relationships with an opportunistic mindset for our own ministry to be recognized. While a good spiritual father or mother may help us go to the next level in our individual destiny or calling, they will also expect a connection and service to a bigger picture.

The Bible says that the elders were to bear the burden with Moses. A profound truth is revealed here. Spiritual fathers and mothers carry a weighty mantle that requires assistance from those in their spiritual family. The apostolic mentality is one of labor and work

The Law of Transfer 57

with divine enablement and anointing. An apostolic company joins together in the fulfillment of the assignment. At this level of impartation, those entrusted with leadership must have completed the necessary homework to get free from past demons, traumas, and every remnant of rejection. They cannot live out of past wounds. Moses gathered the leaders together as an apostolic father. There was a divine transfer of ability, wisdom, and anointing to get the job done. Collectively they formed a complete picture able to lead the masses of people God had entrusted to Moses' ministry.

> Therefore I urge you, brothers and sisters, by the mercies of God, to present your bodies [dedicating all of yourselves, set apart] as a living sacrifice, holy and well-pleasing to God, which is your rational (logical, intelligent) act of worship. And do not be conformed to this world [any longer with its superficial values and customs], but be transformed and progressively changed [as you mature spiritually] by the renewing

of your mind [focusing on godly values and ethical attitudes], so that you may prove [for yourselves] what the will of God is, that which is good and acceptable and perfect [in His plan and purpose for you].

— Romans 12:1-2, AMP

6
IDENTITY IS KEY

Now that we have identified the evil work of rejection and the nature of apostolic relationships, let's examine some key components of our identity in Christ Jesus. In your journey to break free from rejection, the renewing of your mind is crucial. You must break the thought processes and emotions connected with past rejection and trauma, casting out every demon associated with the attack. Cast out, cleanse, and allow the medicine of the Word of God to wash your mind from old wounds and bondages. As you dig deep into the Word of God, you will be redefined by the scriptures. You will shun your old way of thinking, coming to an understanding of the radical love of the Father towards you and knowing Christ more intimately. This realization positions you for glorious freedom!

KEY TRUTHS TO ESTABLISH YOUR HEART TO LIVE FREE FROM REJECTION

1. You have been accepted!

> Blessed be the God and Father of our Lord Jesus Christ, who hath blessed us with all spiritual blessings in heavenly places in Christ: According as he hath chosen us in him before the foundation of the world, that we should be holy and without blame before him in love: Having predestinated us unto the adoption of children by Jesus Christ to himself, according to the good pleasure of his will, to the praise of the glory of his grace, wherein he hath made us accepted in the beloved.
> — Ephesians 1:3-6, KJV

These verses reveal the complete and total sacrifice of Jesus Christ to bring you out of sin and bondage and into the family of God. There are a whole host of scriptures in the New Testament reaffirming this singular truth. It is imperative that you grab onto this verse, meditate on it, and speak it over your life daily. You must allow the Word of God to wash your mind free from all rejection and align you with the promise of God.

2. Your Position in righteousness through faith in the sacrifice of Jesus.

> For he hath made him to be sin for us, who knew no sin; that we might be made the righteousness of God in him.
> —2 Corinthians 5:21, KJV

> Even the righteousness of God which is by faith of Jesus Christ unto all and upon all them that believe: for there is no difference.
> — Romans 3:22, KJV

The enemy will come at you with condemnation and shame from past mistakes or even present shortcomings.

While repentance is a wonderful and renewing ministry of the Holy Spirit, it needs to be empowered with a proper understanding of faith and grace, not law and condemnation. Alignment with the work of Jesus at the cross empowers your right standing with God, which is vital for your life. When you believe in Jesus Christ and stand before God justified by His blood, not your own works, you stand right with the Lord.

3. **The glorious power of Christ's freedom and forgiveness in our lives.**

> If the Son therefore shall make you free, ye shall be free indeed.
> — John 8:36, KJV

> In whom we have redemption through his blood, the forgiveness of sins, according to the riches of his grace.
> — Ephesians 1:7, KJV

By faith in Jesus Christ, there is a place of divine freedom that allows us to stand in the absolute knowledge of God's love for us and His total redemption of our lives. When we align our hearts with these truths, we bind the hand of the enemy in our lives through accusation and condemnation.

4. Jesus Christ came to provide peace for us.

The rejected soul is a tormented one. A person bound with rejection has a daily invasion of negative thoughts, causing emotional turbulence. Yet, there is a place declared in scripture to walk free from such pain and bondage.

> And the peace of God, which passeth all understanding, shall keep your hearts and minds through Christ Jesus.
> — Philippians 4:7, KJV

There is a place of peace that confounds the human mind. A person fully planted in the love of God, the sacrifice of Jesus Christ, and the glorious blood of Jesus can be at emotional rest even in the midst of a crisis or storm. They don't simply have natural peace connected to their present circumstances but are dwelling in a place of rest far greater than that of natural man. This truth needs to be applied to every area of our lives through meditation and confession of the Word of God, prayer, and trusting in the arms of Jesus Christ.

Now that we have walked fully through the description of rejection, the necessity of spiritual relationships, the expectation upon these relationships, and the beautiful promises of God in our lives, let's examine some practical steps to walk free from rejection.

7
DIVINE REMEDIES

Get into the HEALING presence of God!
Receive the glorious healing ministry of Jesus Christ, which is able to permeate your soul with unfathomable freedom. Be intentional in devotion and prayer life to call upon Jesus the Healer of emotions and pains.

Get deliverance!
Allow others with authority to break demonic entities in your life and slam doors shut. Do self-deliverance by commanding demon powers to go and resisting any attempt for them to return. Use the authority of the believer, bought by the blood of Jesus Christ, to keep yourself free from the grips of hell. Remember, David, worshipped his way out.

Identify and confront the strongholds.

Understand behaviors associated with past pain and rejection. Begin to go to work with the Word of God to dismantle the lies of the enemy brick by brick, piece by piece.

Renew your mind!

Take God's Word for your life as daily medicine. Study the scriptures on acceptance and the love of God. Dive deep into the Bible and learn what God says about you. Arm yourself with the truth of the Word of God.

Confront and change behavior patterns.

There are aspects of deliverance that are instantaneous when demons are cast out, but there are deliverances that take time. You must begin to take responsibility for your actions by recognizing unhealthy behavior patterns and confronting them with resistance, authority, and confession of the Word of God.

Give yourself grace to walk out the process.

You may mess up and fall back into old thought processes and behaviors, but don't allow the enemy to condemn you for a temporary mistake. Immediately repent and take authority over any emotional turbulence. With commitment to the power of the Holy Spirit, the written Word of God, the radical love of Jesus, and the arms of your heavenly Father, you can and will overcome rejection!

The gospel message is a great love story written by a lovesick Bridegroom who refused to give up on His bride. He laid it all on the line to ransom the one that He loved. The God of all creation sent His Son to die on a rugged cross for you and me. The depth of love expressed through the Bible is almost unfathomable to the human mind.

To fully grasp the depth of His love requires your spiritual mind to be activated because human emotions and wisdom are limited to natural feelings. It takes our new nature, along with the guidance of Holy Spirit, to come into the awareness of these truths and realize that God has always loved us, will always love us, and continues to love us amid our struggles. The realization and adoption of these truths shatter the yoke of bondage fabricated by the spirit of rejection. You do not have to live bound by rejection, fear, or shame. There is a pathway of glorious freedom for you. There is a place in His everlasting love where you can rest in the arms of your Savior, healed and whole from the past.

> The Lord appeared to me (Israel) from ages past, saying,
> "I have loved you with an everlasting love;
> Therefore with lovingkindness I have drawn you and continued My faithfulness to you.
> — Jeremiah 31:3, AMP

He has loved you!
He paid it all for you!
You are rejected no more!
You are isolated no more!
His love is beckoning you to come and enjoy freedom for your soul, break the chains of bondage, and dwell in the house of your Father. His house is one of grace, love, and mercy.

My prayer over you:

Father, I thank you for my friend.
You see the pain, the shame, and the old bondages, and you surround it all with love.
I pray now that every demon flees!
I command rejection, shame, and pain to go, in the name of Jesus.
I thank you for your great love for my friend.
I thank you for a new pathway and a new way of living.
I thank you for strength, wisdom, and grace coming forth, in the name of Jesus.
I thank you for your everlasting love being released in their heart.
I thank you that they are rejected no more!
You have accepted them in the beloved.
They are adopted, loved, and forgiven, in the name of Jesus.
Amen!